# Le Ly Hayslip

by Mary Englar

Raintree

Chicago, Illinois

© 2006 Raintree
Published by Raintree, a division of Reed Elsevier, Inc.
Chicago, Illinois
Customer Service:  888-363-4266
Visit our website at www.raintreelibrary.com

Printed and bound in china by South China Printing Company Limited.
10 09 08 07 06
10 9 8 7 6 5 4 3 2 1

**Library of Congress Cataloging-in-Publication Data:**
Englar, Mary.
  Le Ly Hayslip / Mary Englar.
     p. cm. -- (Asian-American biographies)
  Includes bibliographical references and index.
   ISBN 1-4109-1055-5 (hc) -- ISBN 1-4109-1128-4 (pb)
  1. Hayslip, Le Ly--Juvenile literature. 2. Vietnamese
Americans--Biography--Juvenile literature. 3. Vietnamese American
women--Biography--Juvenile literature. 4. Refugees--United
States--Biography--Juvenile literature. 5. Vietnamese Conflict,
1961-1975--Biography--Juvenile literature. I. Title. II. Series.
  E184.V53E54 2005
  973'.049592'0092--dc22

                                2005005639

**Acknowledgments**
The publisher would like to thank the following for permission to reproduce photographs:
Corbis pp. 19 (Bettmann), 21 (Hulton-Deutsch Collection), 31 (Bettmann), 34 (Ted Streshinsky), 38 (Nik Wheeler),
44 (Tim Page), 51 (Sygma/Eric Robert), 54 (Sygma/Mark S. Wexler), 57 (Nevada Wier), 58 (Reuters); Courtesy Le Ly
Hayslip pp. 4 (Michael Kaplan), 6, 8, 29, 33, 46, 49, 52 (Geoffrey Clifford), 52b (Phung Van Nghe); Doubleday
Books p. 40 "When Heaven and Earth Changed Places" by Le Ly Hayslip; Magnum Photos pp. 12 (Werner Bischof),
14 (Bruno Barbey), 25 (Bruno Barbey), 26.

Cover photograph: Courtesy Le Ly Hayslip (Michael Kaplan)

Special thanks to Le Ly Haslip and the East Meets West Foundation for their help in the preparation of this book.

Every effort has been made to contact copyright holders of any material reproduced in this book. Any omissions will
be rectified in subsequent printings if notice is given to the publisher

Some words are shown in bold, **like this**. You can find out what
they mean by looking in the glossary.

# Contents

*Le Ly Hayslip has dedicated her life to improving health and education in her native Vietnam.*

# Introduction

In 1989 Le Ly (pronounced "lay lee") Hayslip returned home to her village in Vietnam. She slept in her family's two-room house for the first time in more than 20 years. She came to speak at a celebration to open the first medical clinic ever built in her village. Le Ly had worked hard to raise the money needed to build this clinic. Since opening in 1989, the Mother's Love Clinic has provided free medical services to thousands of Vietnamese people who cannot afford to pay for health care.

The Mother's Love Clinic was the first step in a new career for Le Ly. She wanted to build better relationships between the people of the United States and the people of Vietnam. The Vietnam War took the lives of more than 57,000 American soldiers. The war destroyed much of Vietnam as well. Le Ly's **foundations** have helped to rebuild a small part of what the war destroyed.

Le Ly was born on a farm in Ky La, Vietnam. For much of her childhood, North Vietnam and South Vietnam were fighting a

*The Mother's Love Clinic in Ky La, Vietnam, was opened in 1989.*

**civil war**. Her village was in central Vietnam, and the armies fought battles near Ky La almost every day. It was a terrible and frightening time in Le Ly's life.

When Le Ly was 20 years old, she married an American and **immigrated** to the United States. After the terror of the war, she found new challenges in America. She had to learn to speak English, and she had to learn a new **culture** that was very different from the one she knew. But Le Ly showed courage and **determination** in overcoming the challenges for new **immigrants**. She worked and studied hard to improve her life.

Le Ly wrote two books about her life. She worked hard to start her own restaurant. But Le Ly still worried about her homeland and the destruction left by years of war. She decided to raise money for two charitable **foundations** that build hospitals, children's homes, and schools for the people of Vietnam.

Le Ly believes that she is lucky. More than two million Vietnamese people died during the war. Many more were injured. She saw how war destroyed the countryside and families. Since the war she has met hundreds of Americans and Vietnamese people who want to solve the problems caused by war. Le Ly believes that all people want to help when they see a problem. Her unique skill is that of bringing people together to do good works for people in need.

## In Her Own Words

"If nothing else, wars make you appreciate what's important."

"Today I am very honored to live in the United States and proud to be a U.S. citizen. I do my best to honor the American flag, which I have seen not only raised in battle against me, but flying proudly over the schools where my wonderful boys have learned to be Americans."

"If I've learned one thing from my travels and adventures, it's that the more we respect and value ourselves, the more we respect and value others. No life is worth wasting."

"America picked me up when I was scared ... and cared for me and educated me and helped me raise my three wonderful sons."

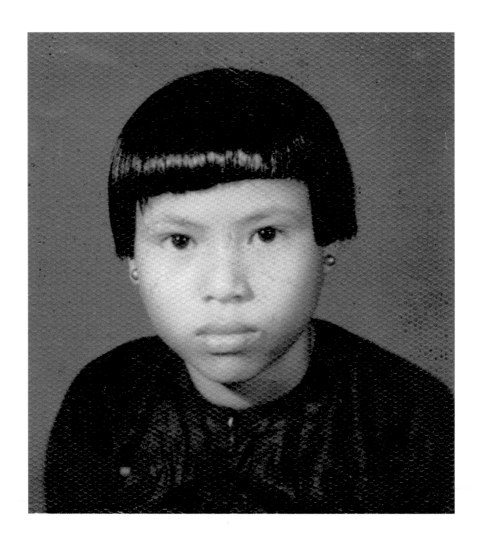

*This photo shows Le Ly Hayslip as a young girl.*

# Chapter 1:
# Growing Up in Vietnam

Phung Thi Le Ly was born in the village of Ky La, Vietnam, on December 19, 1949. Vietnam is a country in Southeast Asia. Ky La was a farming village about 18 miles (30 kilometers) from the coastal city of Da Nang. The village lay at the edge of rice fields, called **paddies**. Hills and jungle surrounded the green valley.

Le Ly's mother Huyen and father Trong owned rice paddies in Ky La. The family's house had two rooms. Le Ly's father slept in the front room. Her mother and the children slept in the back room.

## A Large Family

Le Ly was the youngest of six children. She was born early and weighed only 2 pounds (1 kilogram). Her mother kept Le Ly with her all day while she worked. Huyen talked to her baby and told her to be strong. She milked their water buffalo for milk to feed Le Ly, and soon Le Ly began to grow.

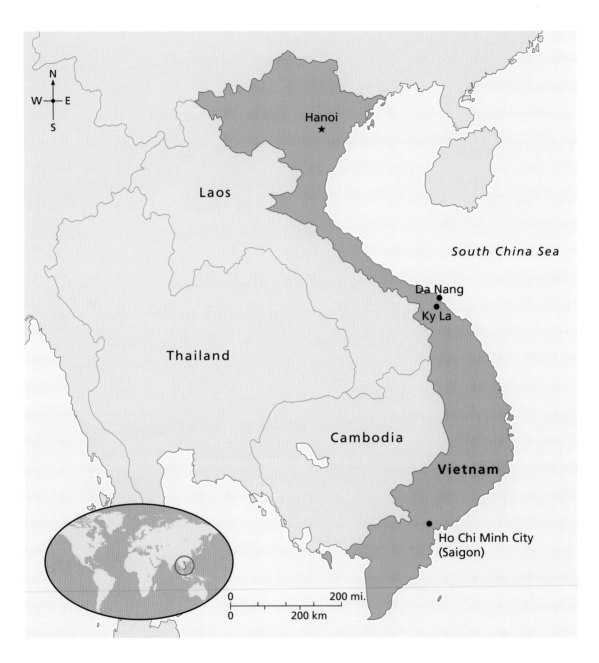

*This map of Vietnam and the surrounding countries shows the major cities in Vietnam and the cities of Ky La and Da Nang.*

As Le Ly got stronger, her mother left her at home with Lan, an older sister, and her brother, Sau Ban. Sau Ban was only five years older than Le Ly was. Her other siblings were her oldest brother Bon Nghe and her sisters, Hai and Ba Xuan.

Everyone in the village depended on rice for their main food. Twice a year they planted rice seeds. Le Ly and the other small children spent all day chasing away birds that came to eat the rice seeds. When the seeds sprouted, the women and girls moved the seedlings to the **paddies**. The paddies were flooded with water from a river and ponds, and the women and girls stood in knee-deep mud to transplant the seedlings. It was very hard work.

When Le Ly got older, she helped her mother pull weeds in the rice paddies. While they worked Huyen taught Le Ly about her duties as a Vietnamese woman. She would have to work hard for her future husband and family. Farming was a difficult life, and Le Ly had to learn how to feed her family even when the rice crop was poor. Le Ly helped her mother to plant a large garden for vegetables. Her mother sold extra vegetables, and ducks when the family needed money.

Le Ly's father Trong was very religious. He was a Buddhist and he taught Le Ly how to practice their religion. Buddhists believe in the teachings of **Buddha**. Trong taught Le Ly that honoring their **ancestors** was her most important duty. He taught her that

*Le Ly's family used a water buffalo to plant seed in the flooded rice paddies.*

Vietnam was the land of her **ancestors**, and so she must always protect the land. Some evenings her father put her on his knee and sang funny songs. All the village children came to listen to her father and his songs.

## The Village School

For several years Le Ly and her older brother, Sau Ban, went to school in the village. They went for four hours in the morning, and three hours in the afternoons. The students learned to read and write at school. Sending children to school was impossible for many villagers. Most of them needed their children to help work in the rice **paddies**.

Le Ly's best memories of Ky La were the few years between the war with France (1946–1954) and the start of a **civil war** (1957) in Vietnam. Ky La had many places to play. After school and in the summer, Le Ly and Sau Ban came home and did their chores. Then they ran out to play with the neighbors. Sometimes they floated boats they made from coconut shells on the ponds. In the hot weather, they swam in the river. These were happy times for her family.

## A New War Begins

Le Ly remembered only a little of the war against the French soldiers that ended when she was five years old. She remembered being afraid of the soldiers and their weapons, and that sometimes her family did not have food to eat. The Vietnamese people were fighting for **independence** from the French. At the end of the war in 1954, the French and the Vietnamese signed a **treaty**. This agreement divided Vietnam into two countries—North and South Vietnam.

*U.S. soldiers landed in small villages to look for Vietcong.*

# Chapter 2:
# War Comes to Ky La

Le Ly remembers one day early in the war. She was taking care of her family's water buffalo out in the fields. The buffalo was eating grass. It was a warm day and Le Ly was daydreaming. In the distance, she heard the sound of a motor. She was used to the sound of **Republican** army trucks by then, so she did not worry about it. But then the noise grew closer and much louder.

Le Ly looked up and saw two green helicopters in the sky above her. They slowly came down to land. The wind from the blades blew off her hat. The buffalo ran away from the noise. Le Ly was so frightened that she dropped to her knees and covered her head. She peeked up to see a stranger climb out of the helicopter and take out binoculars.

Le Ly had never seen such a tall man. The blonde haired man checked the jungle using his binoculars. He did not see Le Ly.

He called out something to the pilot in a strange language. Then the helicopters took off over the tops of the trees.

Le Ly's father ran to get her from the field. Trong was angry. He told her they were dangerous. The helicopters carried American soldiers and weapons. Trong told her she must run away when she saw the dangerous helicopters. This was the first time Le Ly saw Americans in Ky La.

## The United States Sends Soldiers to Vietnam

Soon Le Ly began to see more American soldiers in Ky La. They joined the **Republican** soldiers and searched for **Vietcong** soldiers. Their trucks came along the dirt road into the village. The trucks carried heavy equipment and guns. The United States sent helicopters, planes, boats, soldiers, and weapons to help the Republican soldiers fight the Vietcong soldiers.

Because Ky La was near the border with North Vietnam, Republican soldiers forced the villagers to dig ditches around the village. Then the soldiers put barbed wire along the edge of the jungle. The Republicans wanted to keep the Vietcong out of the village. The soldiers told the villagers to stay in their houses and not burn oil lamps after dark. Le Ly was afraid and confused.

# Vietnam War (1954–1975)

The United States supported France when they were fighting the **communist** army of Ho Chi Minh in Vietnam. The U.S. was afraid that communism would spread all over the world if they did not fight against it. At first, the U.S. sent money and weapons to the French, and then later, to the South Vietnamese. By 1961 U.S. soldiers were training the South Vietnamese army.

The North Vietnamese soldiers were determined to win the war at any cost. By the end of 1965, the U.S. had sent more than 180,000 soldiers to Vietnam. By the end of 1968, more than 500,000 U.S. soldiers were fighting in Vietnam. But even with the large army, the North Vietnamese people did not give up. They were fighting for **independence**.

In the United States many Americans had turned against the war. They **protested** in Washington, D.C., and at universities across the country. In 1973 President Richard Nixon agreed to pull the U.S. soldiers out of Vietnam. The South Vietnamese people continued to fight the North Vietnamese people, but they slowly lost the war. In April 1975 the last Americans left South Vietnam. Almost 100,000 Vietnamese people left Vietnam for the United States in April 1975.

The U.S. lost about 58,000 soldiers during the Vietnam War. Over 300,000 soldiers were wounded, and another 2,500 soldiers were missing. Vietnam believes that more than two million Vietnamese soldiers and citizens died during the war.

The Vietnam War changed the U.S. in many ways. Most of the Vietnamese **immigrants** left their country because they feared for their lives. Some, like Le Ly, chose to immigrate before the war ended. After more than 25 years, Vietnamese Americans have adapted to life in the U.S. But many older immigrants still think of Vietnam as their homeland.

## The Vietcong Soldiers Came at Night

When the **Republican** soldiers did not find any **Vietcong** people in Ky La, they moved on to another village. Then the Vietcong came out of the jungle where they were hiding. They asked the villagers for food and clothing. They called them to meetings in the jungle and explained the war from their point of view. The Vietcong wanted Vietnam to be **independent** of any other country. They wanted freedom for all their people. If the villagers helped the Republicans and Americans, the Vietcong told them they would become slaves to the United States.

Le Ly and her family did not know a lot about either government. They wanted the freedom to grow their crops, stay on their land, and follow their **traditions**. Many villagers helped the Vietcong. Le Ly's brother Bon Nghe was fighting with the North Vietnamese Army (NVA), which fought alongside the Vietcong. The Vietcong used children to take messages between the different groups in the jungle.

Le Ly's job was to warn the Vietcong. She believed she was fighting for freedom and for Vietnam. In some ways, it was a game for the children. They would steal food and weapons from the Americans or **Republicans** and give them to the Vietcong. They were not afraid of getting caught at first. But soon the bombing came closer to Ky La.

*The Vietcong soldiers trained in North Vietnam to fight the Republican Army of South Vietnam.*

## Preparing for War

Le Ly's parents decided to prepare a safe place to hide underground, called a bunker. The bunker protected them from bombs. They dug a deep hole a few feet from their front door. They used cement to make the walls strong, and covered the roof with straw and sand. After it was finished, they brought in oil lamps, a pail of water, blankets, and rice.

Soon the **Republicans** and Americans set up a permanent camp in the village. One night the **Vietcong** attacked. Mortar shells exploded in the middle of the camp. The Americans and Republicans were surprised by the attack. Le Ly was visiting a neighbor when the battle began. She heard the explosions. As she ran home, she saw bright sparks from the soldiers' guns out in the **paddies**. Her family went into the underground bunker. The fighting lasted all night as the Americans and Republicans chased the Vietcong back into the jungle.

The next morning Le Ly and her family crawled out of their bunker. Many villagers and Vietcong soldiers died in the fighting. The villagers began to bury the people who had died. When the American and Republican soldiers came back from the jungle, they went from house to house. They were angry and wanted to find any Vietcong who might be hiding there. If they found anything suspicious, they burned the house and arrested the villagers.

*Many battles in Vietnam were fought in small villages like this one.*

## Too Many Dangers

By 1964 the fighting in and near Ky La was constant. The bombs destroyed the rice **paddies**. All of their animals had been killed. Le Ly and her mother went into the jungle to collect firewood and wild fruit. They sold these things to buy food.

Many children had lost their parents in the fighting. They wandered from house to house looking for food. Le Ly's family shared what they could. By this time more than 60 percent of the villagers had either died, run away to the large cities, or been arrested by the soldiers. Le Ly's father was afraid for his wife and young daughter.

In 1964 **Republican** soldiers arrested Le Ly, who was only fourteen. During a sudden battle in Ky La, Le Ly had jumped into a ditch to escape the bombs. The soldiers accused her of helping the **Vietcong** soldiers. They put Le Ly in jail for three nights. Her sister, Ba Xuan, sent her husband, who was a Republican policeman, to ask for Le Ly's release. The soldiers warned Le Ly before they let her go. If they caught her helping the Vietcong again, she would be put in prison. Le Ly felt lucky that she only spent three nights in jail.

Many people were kept in prison for months. The villagers in Ky La thought she must be a spy for the Republicans. In 1965 her parents sent Le Ly away to live with her sisters in Da Nang. She was 15 years old. She had visited relatives in Da Nang, but she had never lived in a city.

## City Life

For the next five years, Le Ly learned how to live in the city. When she arrived in Da Nang, the United States had built a large military base and hospital there. By the end of 1966, more than 400,000 American soldiers were fighting with the **Republican** Army of South Vietnam. Thousands of people in the country who had lost their homes and farms during the war escaped to Da Nang and other large cities in South Vietnam.

Le Ly found work wherever she could. She worked in a laundry, as a housekeeper, and as a nursing assistant at a hospital. With both Le Ly and her sister Lan working, they were able to pay the rent for a one-room apartment. Le Ly felt lucky to have a place to live. Many homeless people slept on the streets.

Le Ly's sister worked at a restaurant that served many American soldiers when they had a few days off from the fighting. Le Ly got to know some soldiers through her sister. Many of the Americans were just a few years older than she was. Many did not know why they were fighting in Vietnam. Daily life in Da Nang was hard, but Le Ly did not have to worry about the bombing in the countryside anymore.

## Selling Souvenirs

Le Ly began to sell Vietnamese **souvenirs** to American soldiers. She bought **traditional** Vietnamese dresses, jewelry, and crafts and sold them. Before the soldiers returned to the United States, they bought souvenirs for their families They paid Le Ly well, and she began to save money.

In 1966 Le Ly suddenly found herself pregnant. At only 16 years old, she worried about how she would take care of a baby. She gave birth to a son in 1967. She named him Hung. Her mother came to live with her when she had her baby. After a few months, Le Ly's mother took care of Hung, and Le Ly went back to her souvenir business. Now she had to work to feed her new son and her mother, too.

Le Ly worried about keeping her son safe from the war. For most of her life, Vietnam had been at war. She did not want her son to grow up the same way. Anywhere in the world would be safer for her family. Le Ly knew a lot about life in the United States. The soldiers she met told her about their homes. Le Ly began to save money to leave Vietnam.

*Many American soldiers bought souvenirs during the Vietnam War.*

*Le Ly met her first husband Ed Munro in 1969.*

# Chapter 3:
# A New Life in the United States

In 1969 Le Ly was introduced to Ed Munro. He was an American **engineer** who worked for an American construction company in Vietnam. He was much older than Le Ly, but he was kind and interested in her son. Very soon after they met, Ed asked her to marry him. Le Ly was surprised. She was only 19 years old. She dreamed of leaving Vietnam, but she did not know if she wanted to marry a man in his mid-50s. She told Ed she would think about marriage.

Le Ly had trouble deciding to leave her country forever. Family was very important to her. Her father had died suddenly the year before. He was buried in Ky La. Her brother, Sau Ban, had died in the war. No one knew where he was buried. Le Ly's mother and sisters all lived near Da Nang. Le Ly knew her mother would never leave Vietnam, and she had promised her father to honor her **ancestors** and protect their land in Ky La.

But Ed promised her a good life in the United States. He wanted to adopt her son. If Le Ly married Ed, her son would grow up in a safe environment. He could go to school and get a good education. Le Ly wanted a better life for her son. After several months, Le Ly agreed to marry Ed.

## Marriage and a Second Son

Le Ly and Ed were married in Vietnam in 1969. In February 1970, Le Ly and Ed had a son. She named her new son Tommy. When Ed adopted Hung, she gave him the American name Jimmy. Le Ly hoped the American names would help her sons when they started school. Ed flew to San Diego, California, to plan for their arrival. In May 1970, Le Ly and her two sons got on a plane and flew to San Diego. She was only 20 years old and had never been out of Vietnam before.

## Everything in America Was Different

When Le Ly and her sons arrived in San Diego, they stayed with Ed's mother. Le Ly spoke some English, but most of Ed's family spoke too fast for her to understand. Ed's mother had modern appliances that Le Ly had never used. She had to learn to use a dishwasher, washing machine, and garbage disposal.

American food was also different. In Vietnam Le Ly shopped at the market every day for fish and vegetables. She bought rice in 220 pound (100 kilogram) bags. Her family ate rice at every meal.

*Le Ly's home in San Diego contained many objects that reminded her of Vietnam.*

In America rice came in a small box. Ed did not eat rice, so Le Ly learned to cook meat and potatoes for him.

Soon after Le Ly arrived in San Diego, she met some Americans who did not like the Vietnamese people. Many American soldiers had died in the war, and some Americans thought all Vietnamese people were **communists**. When Le Ly went to the grocery store, she felt that the clerk did not like her. Le Ly tried to change her Vietnamese looks. She cut her hair short, bought American clothes, and studied to improve her English.

In 1972 Ed moved his family to a house in the suburbs of San Diego. The neighborhood was so new that there were few trees. Le Ly was excited. She planned a garden and new trees for their house. Jimmy started his first year of school and Le Ly took classes in English. Her teachers were very patient, and Le Ly learned quickly.

A year later, Ed became sick with a bad cold. He died from **pneumonia** a few days later. Le Ly was left alone with house payments, two small children, and no job skills. Ed's family gave her money to help her while she looked for a job. She learned to drive, and took a part-time job as a housekeeper. Le Ly was careful with her money, and she felt proud that she was able to take care of her children on her own.

## The Vietnam War Ends

In 1973 the United States, South Vietnam, and North Vietnam signed the Paris Peace **Treaty** to end the war in Vietnam. North Vietnam agreed to pull their army out of South Vietnam. The United States agreed to send their soldiers home, too. But North Vietnam did not keep the treaty. By 1975 the North Vietnamese took over all of Vietnam and created the Socialist **Republic** of Vietnam.

Le Ly watched the news and worried about her family. She did not know if they were hurt in the fighting. After North Vietnam took over, the United States cut off all communications with Vietnam. Le Ly could not write to her family or receive letters from

*In 1975 Saigon fell to the North Vietnamese army. More than 100,000 Vietnamese tried to escape from Vietnam.*

them. More than 100,000 Vietnamese people left Vietnam after the takeover. Only Le Ly's sister, Lan, left Vietnam. Lan told her that their family was safe, but very frightened. Le Ly helped Lan get started in the United States.

## A Second Marriage

In 1975 Le Ly married Dennis Hayslip. She had known him for several years, and Dennis wanted to help her take care of her sons. They had a son, Alan, in December 1975. The family moved to a large house. Le Ly turned the backyard into a garden. She planted bananas, bamboo, and many kinds of vegetables. The garden reminded her of her mother's garden in Vietnam.

With her two older sons in school, Le Ly had time to write down some stories she remembered her father telling her. The more she wrote about her life in Vietnam, the more she missed her family. She continued to write even though it made her homesick. She wanted to write her life story down for her children. She wrote in Vietnamese on notebook paper and kept the writings in a box.

*Le Ly married her second husband, Dennis Hayslip, in 1975.*

*Le Ly worked on an assembly line like this one.*

# Chapter 4:
# Her Own Business

Le Ly worked many different kinds of jobs after she came to the United States. At one job she worked on a computer assembly line. There she met many Vietnamese women. Most had left Vietnam after 1975, but others were married to Americans. They talked while they worked, and Le Ly made some friends.

Vietnamese Americans often help each other financially when they want to start a business. Le Ly and her friends started a money-saving group similar to ones that were common in Vietnam. Every month the group members put a certain amount of money together to help one member start a business. One member then asked for the money when they had a good idea. The money was used for new restaurants, jewelry shops, and sewing businesses. When the business was making money, the group member paid back the money.

In 1980 Le Ly decided to ask for the group's money to buy a small deli. The deli was located in a neighborhood where many **immigrants** lived. She had learned how to run a business from her work in Vietnam. She was certain she could make money and pay back her friends.

Le Ly did not ask Dennis if she could start her own business. When he found out, he was very angry. He wanted her to take care of the house and children. Le Ly wanted her own business, but her disagreement with her husband bothered her. In Vietnam a wife was expected to obey her husband. Le Ly decided to give up her business and pay back the money.

In 1982 Dennis died in an accident. He fell asleep in his van while it was still running. The gas fumes from a charcoal heater killed him. Once again Le Ly was left alone to raise her sons. This time, Dennis had left insurance money. Le Ly had some money to support her family, but she knew she would have to find a job.

## Learning the Restaurant Business

After Dennis died Le Ly started thinking again about her own business. One of the women she knew from her old computer assembly job was working at a new Chinese restaurant. One day, Le Ly and some friends had lunch there. The food was very good, but the waitresses were young and disorganized.

Le Ly talked to the owner about giving her a job. She offered to work for two weeks for no money. If business did not improve in that time, he did not have to hire her. But if it did, she wanted to be the manager. The new owner, who was also the cook, agreed to let her try. Le Ly organized the dining room so the waitresses could move around easily. She checked out customers quickly so they did not have to wait. She learned the names of the customers and their favorite meals.

After two weeks, Le Ly had shown the owner how she could help him. He hired her to manage the restaurant. She learned how to hire and schedule new employees. She greeted customers by name and welcomed them with good service and good food. She also looked for ways to help the owner keep expenses down.

## Her Own Restaurant

After Le Ly had worked for six months, she was ready to start her own restaurant. She found a space for the restaurant, but she did not have enough money to get started. She went to the owner of the Chinese restaurant and told him she was going into business for herself. He offered to be a partner and put up part of the money for her to get started. Her boss knew how hard she worked and that she would be successful.

*The Hollylinh restaurant served traditional Vietnamese dishes like these.*

## The Hollylinh Restaurant

In 1985 Le Ly opened her new restaurant in Temecula, just south of Los Angeles. It took three months to get the restaurant decorated and to hire workers. Le Ly greeted her customers and kept her workers happy. She was very busy, but the restaurant did well. One day a group of people came in and asked for her by name. She talked to them about Vietnam, and they were very happy with their food.

Le Ly did not know it, but the group were all reporters for the local newspaper. They loved her restaurant and wrote a very good review. As soon as the review was published, the phone began to ring with new customers calling for reservations. The review brought people to the Hollylinh from many nearby towns.

The review also told about her life in Vietnam. About two weeks after the review was in the newspaper, a small group of men came into the restaurant and asked for Le Ly. The men told her they were **veterans** of the Vietnam War and wanted to know more about the Vietnamese people. They asked questions about Vietnamese **culture**, and Le Ly enjoyed sharing what she knew with them.

Not everyone that heard about her life in Vietnam was happy to meet her. Some Vietnam veterans did not like it that she had helped the **Vietcong**. These veterans had spent a year of their lives fighting the Vietcong. When North Vietnam took over South Vietnam in 1975, many American veterans felt they had fought for a losing cause. After so many years and the deaths of many of their fellow soldiers, they were still angry about the war.

Le Ly understood why some veterans were angry. She talked to anyone who came in and explained the war was terrible for the Vietnamese people, too. Many veterans enjoyed talking about Vietnam. For the others she felt sad that ten years after the war ended, so many Americans were still angry. She wondered how she might help the veterans get over their anger.

*Le Ly's first book was published in 1989.*

# Chapter 5:
# Le Ly's First Book

For many years Le Ly wrote down stories from her life and saved them. It took her hours to write a couple of pages. In elementary school, she had learned to write only words about life in a farming village. In 1982 she took out the stories and read them. If she wanted to write about all of her life, she would need help.

Le Ly bought a computer for her son Jimmy, who was 15, to use for his homework. He quickly learned how to use it. One day, she asked him if he could **translate** her stories and type them in English. Neither of them knew how hard this would be. But Jimmy found that by typing his mother's story, he learned more about his early life in Vietnam.

After he finished **translating** her writing, Le Ly began to tell him stories in English. He typed her words as she talked. They worked whenever they had time. At the end of the summer of 1985, Jimmy had typed 300 pages.

## Learning About the Publishing Business

Now that Le Ly had a book, she had no idea what to do next. She went to the library and got a list of 100 **publishers**. She sent her book to all of the publishers. Over the next several weeks, she got turned down by many of the publishers. Some were polite and explained that they did not publish books like hers. Others wrote that they did not think Americans were ready to read about the unpopular war.

But Le Ly did not give up. She heard that the University of California at San Diego was holding a conference for writers. She applied for the conference and sent them part of her book. She met many writers, editors, and publishers at the conference. They offered her advice on how to improve her book.

# Return to Vietnam

Before she could finish her book, Le Ly wanted to return to Vietnam to see her family and her village. In 1986 she began to plan her visit. The United States still did not have a relationship with Vietnam, so no airlines flew there. She had to get **permission** from the government in Vietnam. To do this Le Ly had to go through the **United Nations**. As soon as she got permission, she bought a plane ticket to Bangkok, Thailand. From there she could fly into Vietnam.

Le Ly was given permission for a two-week visit to her family. When her Vietnamese friends in America heard about her trip, they were very worried. The government in Vietnam was very dangerous for people who did not agree with them. But Le Ly had not seen her family for nearly 13 years.

In April 1986 Le Ly returned to Vietnam for the first time since a short stay in 1971. She did not know what to expect. She had heard many terrible stories about the Vietnamese government. The Vietnamese **officials** allowed her to visit Da Nang, but they forbid her to go to Ky La. In Da Nang she stayed with a niece. She got together with her sisters, and saw her brother, Bon Nghe, for the first time in 30 years. Her sisters brought her mother to Da Nang from Ky La.

*When Le Ly returned to Vietnam in 1986, she was shocked by the many Vietnamese who had suffered during and after the war.*

The family ate together and Le Ly showed them pictures of her sons. Her brother worked for the government. As he showed her around Da Nang, Le Ly was surprised at the number of people begging in the streets. Many children were missing legs from stepping on old land mines. Le Ly's mother told her that everyone was still afraid. Le Ly wondered what one person could do to help.

## Finishing Her Book

After Le Ly returned from Vietnam, she began to look for a writer to help her rewrite her book. She wanted to add the stories about her return trip, and she felt Jimmy was too busy at college. She finally found an author, Jay Wurts, she trusted. He helped her write an outline to send to **publishers**. Once the project was accepted, Jay would help her finish the book.

In 1987 a publisher in New York accepted Le Ly's book. In May 1989 her first book, *When Heaven and Earth Changed Places*, was published. Le Ly went on a book tour and talked to many audiences about her life. She was shy about her accent, but the audiences welcomed her.

A few months later, her book was sold to publishers in several foreign countries. It was a great success. Before she wrote her book, only American reporters and soldiers had written about Vietnam. Le Ly's book was the first book about the Vietnam War that told what the war was like for ordinary Vietnamese people.

*Le Ly held meetings in her own home in order to get the East Meets West foundation started.*

# Chapter 6:
# The East Meets West Foundation

Le Ly made a second trip to Vietnam in 1988. She talked to government **officials** when she was there. She told them she wanted to help the farmers in the countryside recover from the war. When she returned to the United States, Le Ly began to study **charities** to see how they raised money.

Le Ly volunteered for charity dinners and other events. She learned how charities raised money. She also learned how charities attracted people who wanted to **donate** money or time to help people in need. After she learned what she needed to know, she hired a lawyer to help her start a charitable **foundation** of her own. Le Ly called the new organization East Meets West.

## Veterans Vietnam Restoration Project

The same year Le Ly was contacted by a group of Vietnam **veterans** who offered to help her get started. The veteran who created the Veterans Vietnam Restoration Project was Fredy Champagne. Fredy and Le Ly shared ideas for projects that would help Vietnam the most. Not long after they met, Fredy called to tell her he received **permission** from the Vietnam government to build a medical clinic in Vietnam.

Fredy raised the money and found other veterans who wanted to return to Vietnam. The veterans wanted to help Vietnam rebuild from the war. Fredy's clinic was finished in 1989. The veterans volunteered their time and the Vietnamese government provided the materials.

Fredy and Le Ly planned the next project together. She wanted to build a medical clinic in Ky La. They traveled to Vietnam and met with government **officials** to get permission to work in Vietnam. Fredy showed them the plans for the small clinic that he had finished. The officials agreed that it was a good plan.

## Raising Money

Le Ly had government permission to build her clinic, but she did not have enough money. She returned to the United States. Le Ly used the skills she had learned working for other **charities**. She called people and asked for money. She cooked large Vietnamese

*Fredy Champagne and Le Ly traveled to Vietnam to help get the medical clinic built in Ky La.*

meals for fundraising dinners. Le Ly wrote to everyone she knew and sent information about her **foundation**. But she could not raise all of the money.

About this time, a movie director, Oliver Stone, called Le Ly. He planned to make her book into a movie. Le Ly met with the director. He was a Vietnam **veteran**, and he talked to her for a long time about what he could do in a movie about her life. Le Ly thought about how movies reach a large audience. She imagined it would help her with raising money for her foundation. She agreed that he would make a good movie. After they met, Stone **donated** the rest of the money she needed for the clinic in Ky La.

In September 1989 the new Mother's Love Clinic was finished. Le Ly returned to Ky La for the grand opening. The Red Cross and the Vietnamese Health Department sent **officials** to the opening. Doctors and nurses who would work in the new clinic came from Da Nang. Le Ly stayed in her family's house with her mother and sister.

Everyone in the village came to hear Le Ly speak. Her mother and brother stood in the back row. Le Ly thanked everyone who helped make her dream come true. She told the villagers that Americans were not their enemies. The clinic showed that the Americans wanted to help the people of Vietnam. Le Ly hoped the Vietnamese people and the Americans would become friends

*This picture shows Le Ly (right) with Oliver Stone. On the left is Hiep Thi Le, who played Le Ly in the movie.*

through the work of her foundation.

## Just the Beginning

Le Ly continued to raise money for East Meets West projects. She worked with Fredy's veterans on a large project just outside of Da Nang. It is called Peace Village and is located on China Beach. The project offers medical care for poor and disabled people. The medical center cares for more than 700 patients a day.

*The East Meets West foundation helped to build the Village of Hope orphanage in Da Nang in 1993.*

In 1993 East Meets West helped to build an orphanage in Da Nang. Today more than 180 children live at the Village of Hope. They receive free medical and dental care. All students go to school to learn English, music, and computers. The students also receive job training in sewing, motorcycle repair, and farming.

East Meets West has raised money for many other projects since 1989. The **foundation** has helped to build more than 60 new elementary schools in rural Vietnamese villages. In 1996 the foundation set up a free dental clinic in Da Nang. American dentists volunteered to train Vietnamese dentists and assistants. They also **donated** dental supplies and equipment. The foundation is also working on providing clean water for rural villages. So far they have built more than 40 community wells, and helped plan large water systems for 22 hospitals and villages.

With Le Ly's ideas and **determination**, East Meets West grew from the first clinic in Ky La to a very large organization. The United States government and many Americans have donated money and medical supplies to help the Vietnamese people recover from the war. East Meets West is now the largest **charitable** foundation working in Vietnam.

*Le Ly spent four months on the movie watching Stone film scenes from her childhood.*

# Chapter 6:
# Helping Vietnam Rebuild

After Le Ly's first book about her life in Vietnam was published, she started writing a second book. With Jimmy's help she wrote about her life in the United States. The new book started when Le Ly arrived in San Diego and ended when the clinic in Ky La opened. This second book, titled *Child of War, Woman of Peace*, was published in 1993.

## Making a Movie

At the same time as her second book was published, Le Ly traveled to Thailand to watch as Oliver Stone filmed a movie about her life. She spent more than four months with the crew and actors. The young actress that played Le Ly came from the same area in Vietnam as Le Ly. Though Stone changed some things about her life, Le Ly believed Stone made an honest movie that showed how hard the war was for the Vietnamese people. The movie, *Heaven and Earth*, was released in 1994.

## The Global Village Foundation

In 1999 Le Ly left East Meets West and created a new **foundation** to work on rural education. The Global Village Foundation works to save **traditional** Vietnamese **culture** in rural villages. Le Ly hopes the traditional arts, crafts, music, and dance can be passed on to Vietnam's children. At the same time, she is working on markets for the villagers to sell their crafts and perform their music and dance in Vietnam and around the world.

At first Le Ly invited a group of teachers, students, and **charitable** workers to come to Vietnam to see what needed to be done. After this many from the group returned to Vietnam as volunteers to help with schools, job training, and construction projects. One project in Ky La uses older Vietnamese people to train the young in traditional crafts. The students learn how to sew and make pottery. They are also learning how to make traditional furniture from bamboo.

## New Relationship Between the United States and Vietnam

In 1997 President Bill Clinton sent the first U.S. **ambassador** to Vietnam since the war ended in 1975. Not long after this, the United States began to allow trade and business partnerships with Vietnam. In 2001 Le Ly's foundation began to sell village crafts in the United States. By selling the crafts in the United States, Le Ly found a new way for villagers to make money.

*Le Ly hopes to create markets for traditional crafts in Vietnam and the United States.*

*When President Clinton visited Vietnam in 2000, he became the first American president to go to Vietnam since the war ended in 1975.*

A better relationship between the governments of the United States and Vietnam has helped Le Ly's **foundation** in many ways. Now volunteers can fly directly into Vietnam. The increase in tourism helps the country rebuild their hotels and restaurants. This gives foundation volunteers a place to stay while they are working on a project. As more people visit Vietnam as tourists, more become interested in the projects that Le Ly works on.

Much has changed in Le Ly's life since she left Vietnam in 1970. As a Vietnamese American, she has achieved many great things. Her new foundation hopes to bring **cultures** together to do good works. In 2003 Le Ly started raising money to build a Global Peace Village in southern California. Her new dream is to bring the best of Asian cultures to Americans.

The Global Peace Village will be a place for Americans, Asians, and Asian Americans to come together for food, music concerts, and plays. Le Ly hopes to include many countries from Asia, such as Thailand, Laos, Korea, and Indonesia as well as Vietnam at the new park. For Le Ly, this will be one more achievement in a life devoted to bringing cultures together to make the world a better place.

# Glossary

**ambassador** person sent to a foreign country to represent his or her own country

**ancestor** family member that lived a long time ago

**Buddha** philosopher from India who founded the religion of Buddhism. Buddhism is a religion that teaches duties of honoring ancestors and doing good deeds to improve one's mental and spiritual health.

**charity** organization that raises money to help people in need

**civil war** war between different groups of people in the same country

**colony** one country that is controlled by another country

**communism** system of government where all property is owned by the government, and all people have an equal share of the land and businesses

**culture** stage, form, or kind of civilization

**determination** firmness

**donate** to give money or goods to a charity

**engineer** person who works in engineering, which is a science in which natural energy and properties of matter are used to construct things that are useful to humans, such as structures, machines, and products

**foundation** organization that gives money to help people in need

**immigrate** to come to a new country to become residents. A person who comes to a new country to live is called an immigrant.

**independence** freedom from outside control or support

**official** person who holds an office or is in charge of something

**paddy** wet field where rice is grown

**permission** act of allowing

**pneumonia** serious disease that causes the lungs to fill up with fluid making breathing difficult

**protest** to disapprove or complain about something

**publisher** business that buys, prints, and sells books

**republic** system of government where the people choose their leaders

**Republican** soldiers of South Vietnam were called Republicans

**souvenir** object that people keep to remind them of a special place, person, or event

**tradition** handing down of information, beliefs, or customs from one generation to the next

**translate** to change from one language or set of symbols into another

**treaty** agreement between two or more countries to settle a conflict

**United Nations** international organization created after World War II to help maintain peace in the world

**veteran** someone who has served in the armed forces

**Vietcong** soldiers of North Vietnam involved in the communist movement

# Timeline

| | |
|---|---|
| 1949 | Le Ly is born in Ky La, Vietnam, on December 19. |
| 1954 | French–Indochinese War ends. Vietnam is divided into a North and South Vietnam. Le Ly's oldest brother joins the North Vietnamese Army. |
| 1963 | Le Ly sees the first helicopter in Ky La. |
| 1964 | Le Ly is arrested for spying for the North Vietnamese. |
| 1965 | Le Ly's father sends her to Da Nang to live with her sister. |
| 1967 | First son, Hung, is born. |
| 1969 | Le Ly marries Ed Munro. He adopts Hung. Le Ly gives Hung the American name Jimmy. |
| 1970 | Second son, Tommy, is born in February. Le Ly and her sons leave Vietnam to join Ed in San Diego in May 1970. |
| 1973 | Ed dies. Le Ly finds work as a housekeeper. |
| 1975 | Le Ly marries Dennis Hayslip. Third son, Alan, born in December. South Vietnam falls to North Vietnam. |
| 1982 | Dennis dies accidentally in March. |
| 1985 | Le Ly opens her own restaurant, the Hollylinh. |
| 1986 | Le Ly returns to Vietnam for the first time in 15 years. |
| 1987 | Le Ly creates East Meets West Foundation. |
| 1989 | Her first book is published in May. Mother's Love Clinic opens in Ky La. |
| 1993 | Her second book is published. |
| 1994 | Oliver Stone's movie about Le Ly's life, *Heaven and Earth*, is released. |
| 1999 | Le Ly founds the Global Village Foundation. |

# Further Information

## Further Reading

Dunn, John M. *The Vietnam War*: *A History of U.S. Involvement*. San Diego: Lucent Books, Inc., 2001.

Hall, Margaret C. *Vietnamese Americans*. Chicago: Heinemann Library, 2003.

Rutledge, Paul. *Vietnamese in America*. Minneapolis: Lerner Publications, 1987.

Schmidt, Jeremy. *Two Lands, One Heart*: *An American Boy's Journey to his Mother's Vietnam*. New York: Walker & Co., 1995.

Springstubb, Tricia. *The Vietnamese Americans*. San Diego: Lucent Books, Inc., 2002.

Willis, Terri. *Vietnam*. New York: Children's Press, 2002.

## Addresses

**East Meets West Foundation**
P.O. Box 29292
Oakland, CA 94604

**Embassy of the Socialist Republic of Vietnam**
1233 20th Street N.W., Suite 400
Washington, D.C. 20036

**Global Village Foundation**
P. O. Box 13656
Carlsbad, CA 92013-0656

# Index